Love is the A Matter wh Question

By

Mido Hamada

"If you want to find the secrets of the universe, think in terms of energy, frequency and vibration."

Nikola Tesla

The First Seven Years

Now to be honest, I have absolutely no clue whether this is true or not, but since we live in a free choice world, why not choose "love is the answer no matter what the question" as one's life motto! Of course, there is that pesky little thing called conditioning that keeps me from actually doing this and would rather have me going round in circles, than growing, being happy and living a prosperous life. Know what I mean, what's one to do?

Well, please allow me to introduce myself. For the last twenty plus years, I have worked as an actor in theatre, film and television and subsequently have realised that there are quite a few parallels between the real and the imagined. More on that later because my hypnotherapist told me that it's the first seven years of your life that determines the majority of your conditioning and well, if she said it, then of course it must be true.

Let's begin by looking back at those first seven years, which I now know have such a huge influence over your life.

A long time ago in the desert of the Pharaohs, ah, check that, wrong story!

I was born in Africa, to an abusive father and a slightly mad mother. Repeatedly, I witnessed violence towards my mother which of course, eventually spilled over to me, resulting in the loss of sight in one of my eyes, due to me being punched down the stairs. During this time period, I witnessed my mother's first suicide attempt, which came completely out of the blue for me and deeply shocked and disturbed me. After making a full recovery, she packed our bags in the middle of the night and we fled to Europe.

After a couple of blissful and happy years with just my mother and I, my father eventually found us. This resulted in my mother's second suicide attempt. Miraculously he somehow got the message and left back to Africa, only to return a short time later to kidnap me in the hope of luring my mother and I back home. Luckily, the European police had something to say about that and captured us before we could leave their shores. He was expelled back to Africa and I was returned to my mother. Those were my first seven years.

What do you think I was conditioned with?

Fear! That's right, I said it.

My conditioning was fight or flight, because everything was seen through the lens of that fear conditioned little kid. It had seeped into my subconscious, that this is what life had to offer me, pain, suffering, but most of all, INJUSTICE!

Racism was a daily occurrence, my only escape, the only thing I seemed to be any good at, was sport. Here, I could escape and lose myself in competition.

It wasn't all bad all the time of course. Very quickly I realised that the one ingredient I was never missing in life, was love! Love was always there from my mother, to friends, teachers and coaches; I was always loved.

I have come to the understanding that these are just stories within the story of my life. Life is a movie after all and my father played the part of the villain of my childhood. Now, can I really blame him for playing his part so well? Or do I go on and live my life in happiness and bliss because I realised that there was nothing to forgive, it was just a chapter in my life movie.

Judgement and Self-Righteousness

The direct result of injustice and I don't think we need to go over whether racism, domestic violence etc. is right or wrong, is that it's easy to justify judging those who commit these acts. However, I would like to invite you to challenge that judgement because if we judge them, we join their frequency, which is energy and by so doing we lower our frequency and match theirs. We now have become them, energetically speaking, but hold on, how? We are right! Racism, domestic violence is wrong! How can we now be the same as them? Because "everything is energy and energy is everything and energy cannot be created or destroyed, only transferred or transmuted", Albert Einstein's words, not mine. Rightly or wrongly, by judging them, we are now on the same frequency as them.

By allowing ourselves to judge them, we have allowed those who judge us to transfer their judgemental energy on to us! Especially if we have looked into their eyes, allowing them to directly transfer their energy to our soul. Eyes being the window to the soul and everything…

The most powerful energy in the moment always wins. It's here that we have been conditioned by Hollywood and its endless happy endings, that good always prevails. Right over wrong, good versus evil, light defeating the dark.

That's just not the case. Look around you, is that what you see in your reality? Does that reflect real life? No, not for me, you or anybody on this planet. It's all about choices, moment to moment. You have to choose whom you serve, so to speak, "the light or the dark side of the force", to use Yoda's words! The moment you feel justified and go into self-righteous mode, you gotta know who you are serving! And it ain't Yoda.

If you have never come across Dr David R. Hawkins book Power versus Force, it's worth having a look at his Map of Consciousness. He states that shame, guilt, apathy, grief, fear, desire, anger and pride represent the lower frequency range in regard to your consciousness. Any of those feelings sound familiar? Of course, we have all been there, felt those feelings and sat and wallowed in them. But those feelings are not actually ours, they are not inside us, at all.

What do I mean by that?

Allow me to explain by using the acting process.

Once, I was cast as the villain in a war movie and had to do some incredibly disturbing acts while playing this maniacal character who, at one point, did some horribly violent things to a child. Now, as I woke up that beautiful morning to shoot that particular scene, in the five-star hotel that they had booked us into, not at any point was I feeling particularly maniacal. And as I went down for breakfast and the extremely friendly hotel staff and I interacted in pleasant chit chat, I was still not feeling maniacal. So, the other actors and I catch a ride to set and chat along about this and that without ever talking about the upcoming scene. Shit, still not feeling maniacal.

Now, I'm in my trailer, fully dressed and ready to go, when there is a knock on my door. It's the child actor and his parents, you know the one that I will do horribly violent things to in about ten minutes from now. The whole family is right there standing at my door, with huge smiles and teddy bears in their hands, for me to take home to my family. Seriously, you have got to be freaking kidding me! Where am I gonna get maniacal from now?

So, here I am on set and the director comes over and nods in my direction, which means, your turn now, don't fuck up kid! Cause I'm great at reading minds, no really, I am.

Alright time to earn my money; in my head things are happening that are making me connect to the necessary lower frequency emotions that I will need to play this particular scene. As I've explained, I have not been feeling any of these emotions at all, up to this point. I have to now conjure them up in my head, grasping things from outside of myself, that are not in the least bit real, to be believable as the character for the viewing audience. My body has no idea that this is all pretend because my mind is giving it clear commands and it can't tell the difference between acting and real life. Physically, I AM now in fight or flight mode.

In real life we act the same way. An outside trigger occurs which we react to with the predominant lower frequency we connected to during the conditioning period of our first seven years. It's automated, unconscious in real life, as opposed to conscious and directed during acting. Actors understand which frequency they need to connect to, in order to underline the scene, to then be free and respond moment to moment.

We all need to become conscious in real life, so that we can choose which frequency to answer the trigger with. We need to become actors in our movies, who understand what is really occurring and choose how to react moment to moment, rather than automated and unconscious and therefore allowing our emotions to control us. Hopefully, our choice will be that of the higher frequencies as mentioned in Hawkins's Map of Consciousness - courage, acceptance, reason, love, joy, peace and enlightenment etc.

In my humble opinion, mastery of life means mastery of emotions. To answer any situation like the great sages before us, with love and forgiveness. The choice, in the end, is always between love and fear, your conditioning determines your response. Your level of consciousness, the frequency you choose.

So how do we do it? How do we wake up in our own life movie? How do we start to respond to any life situation with higher frequencies only? How do we stop creating separation between ourselves and others?

By realising we are actually in a movie of our life.

A simulation.

Simulation

Hold on…a simulation, what in God's name does that even mean? Trust me, I'm under no illusion as to my expertise in any of this. But here are my two cents worth never the less.

We are multi-dimensional light beings who are having an earthly experience, in the hope that our consciousness evolves during a succession of life times to the point when we solely exist on those higher frequencies I've mentioned before and discontinue to engage in lower frequency behaviour, whether by thought, word or action. At this point, we either cease to come back, or come back solely for the benefit of humanity as a whole, since the personal karma linked to that specific light entity has been resolved. Graduation from class, so to speak.

The main unit of our consciousness resides in a different dimension, with a much higher frequency, along with the computer or projector (for lack of a better word) that creates and shapes this beautiful movie we are in, called our current life. Our body is nothing more than an avatar which houses a tiny individual unit of said consciousness, which was separated from its main unit of consciousness in another dimension and has completely forgotten who or from where it came. Its sole purpose is to evolve through the use of free choice. You see, we have to choose the higher frequency emotions from moment to moment, by constantly being aware that we have a choice to serve either "the light or the dark side of the force", again Yoda's words not mine. The choices this individual unit of consciousness chooses, determines the future of the avatar, moment to moment.

But here is where all the drama starts...

The avatar comes into existence with, let's call it ego or a sense of itself, limited only to this particular avatar, with a life span that starts at its birth and finishes at its death. Its sole purpose is survival and it can only survive on those said lower frequencies, which were conditioned into it during the avatar's first seven years.

This is the battle, the ego of your avatar against your higher self in another dimension.

You're either serving your ego, your lower self connected to the dark side of the force, or you're serving your higher self connected to the light side of the force. Your choices decide whom you serve - no right or wrong here by the way, but that's a whole different matter. It's our ignorance as to who we truly are and what we should be connecting to, that causes all the strife in our life.

It's my understanding that the whole point is to become awake during our current life movie and look straight into the camera at our higher self and say, gotcha! If you are now thoroughly confused, no worries I feel you!

Let's try this; I was once sitting in a movie theatre with a bunch of agents etc, trust me not the first people that come to my mind to be watching a movie with, that I happened to be in. For some inexplicable reason, I was the only actor there, really awkward! Now, here I was, watching myself on screen going through these very extreme emotions, while the real me was squirming in my seat, wishing I was anywhere but there. It occurred to me that I was watching this character played by me going through all this shit. Me, as in the higher self, sitting in this movie theatre watching my lower self playing a part in this story, without any knowledge that I'm actually watching him. I want to keep yelling at him, "No not there, go left! Stay away from that guy and don't ever trust her!" But like the idiot he is, he has no idea I exist and he never looks straight into camera and asks for my help, seeing that I can see the bigger picture and all. That is until he eventually does look straight into camera and says, "Gotcha! Now please tell me how to play?"

Well, first we have to take care of Leroy.

Leroy

What who?

11

Leroy!

Well for me, and I might be showing my age here, that is the guy from the TV show "Fame", you know, the really talented but unconventional dancer who just had this marvellous mischievous streak. He couldn't help himself but always somehow got into trouble, well, cause rules, you know, they suck! That guy!?

When I think of that character, it always puts an instant smile on my face, so I have decided to call my ego, you know that thing that comes attached to my body avatar and responds solely to those negative frequencies it was conditioned with from my first seven years, Leroy.

Because, as I mentioned earlier, I believe these negative emotions are outside of us and we have to give them permission, so to speak, to enter our bodies. Our conditioning usually allows this energy straight in, but if we name it, with a name that for some reason evokes a smile from us, then we can play with this negative energy and tell it to stay the fuck out! Which goes something like this;

I'm driving down the motorway on a beautiful sunny day, when suddenly some guy dangerously cuts me off. As I am about to burst into an expletive ridden tirade, I remember that I am awake in this life movie and instead I say, "Really Leroy, really?" The sun is shining, you just made love to your wife and the meeting you're driving to is gonna be fantastic but no, go right ahead and let some random bad driving guy, control you and lower your frequency!

Nah, I don't think so.

Not today, Leroy, not today.

I'm just going to continue driving and focus on my own frequency and keep it joyful and loving. The random bad driving guy, will have zero power over me today.

I have found, being direct and sometimes even abrupt but always laced with humour is the best and easiest way to deal with Leroy.

Or if that doesn't work for you, here is another example.

My son, unbeknownst to me, has his own thoughts and dare I say it, quite a few of them, and for some, to me inexplicable reason, doesn't answer me, even though I have now asked for the fifth time if he has cleaned his teeth. I know, I know, I'm a bad parent because I already started to react at five, forgive me, I'm working on it. As my blood starts to boil and it's about to spill over, I remember;

Hey Leroy, really? You are about to go off on a little kid because he can't get his head out of a book and hasn't heard you. Come on Leroy, wow, this is who you are? A bully who has to scare a kid to attention?

Trust me, try this and see if you still go off.

I bet those negative emotions that want to enter you, will be dissolved through your humour. Funny things happen when you give scary things, funny names. All of a sudden, they lose all their power! Negativity, especially that early, deeply conditioned kind, needs to be confronted head on. Again, I don't know this, it's just my opinion. Playing with Leroy, is how I do it. Try it and see for yourself.

So now, we have a grasp over our ego, by naming it and confronting it with humour and lots of love. We start to feel like we connect less and less to those negative emotions, however when we go out into the real world and interact with people, we still feel disconnected. How can we bridge that gap? How about by saying to everyone you meet, "I love me".

I Love Me

No, not out loud, in your head, silly.

And before all the narcissists start screaming, oh, this chapter's for me, cause it is for you and everybody else too. Allow me to explain:

Our main unit of consciousness, in another dimension, is part of the consciousness that is everything, whether you want to call that god, the creator, source or whatever feels right to you. Meaning your main unit of consciousness along with everyone else's main units of consciousness, are part of the consciousness that is everything, which for ease of understanding I will from now on refer to as the Creator.

Alright, back to us in this beautiful dimension of ours.

Our body avatar is governed by an individual unit of consciousness which now, thanks to our increased awareness moment to moment, is only operating on those higher frequencies. So now we go out into the world and have to meet those other human beings, you know the ones that come in all different shapes, sizes, genders, races, religions, sexual orientation, nationalities and, bear with me here, different opinions than our own. But trust me, when you cut us open, we all bleed in the same colour, we are all human. On top of that, we all stem from the same consciousness that is everything, which has syphoned itself off into these individual units of consciousness that you now experience as yourself and the people around you.

We are all one, get it?

This is where I love me comes in.

Once again, I'll use an acting technique to explain.

Sometimes nerves can be a very tricky thing and can rip you out of the moment, the result being, you are completely in your head and very much out of the moment. Not the best place to start a scene from. In these anxiety riddled times, it helps to place all your attention on your scene partner, notice everything about them, really notice them, feel them, what are they going through, what might be afflicting them, really see them, and how and what you can do to help them. The result is that now, all your attention has been placed on your scene partner, your brain's moved on from your anxiety and you are good to go, play the scene and do your job.

Back to real life; pick the most irritating person in your life. Next time you meet that person, really look at them, notice everything about them without commenting or judging, as in, her hair is blond, his nose is wide, as simple as that. Now, remember those eyes that are staring back at you belong to an individual unit of consciousness which is connected to a main unit of consciousness in another dimension. Both your own and the irritating one's main units of consciousness, stem from the consciousness that is everything, the Creator. Now, say in your head, "I love me, I love me" keep repeating it for a bit. Because deep down you recognise that we all come from the same place and are now having this earthly experience for the sake of our evolution but in reality, we are all one.

Just say "I love me", in your head, and allow the magic to happen with this realisation. Say it to everyone and I mean everyone you meet, have met and will ever meet. And see if you still get irritated by anyone.

I love me, because we are all one.

We Are All One

Isn't it annoying when all these new age people spout off, "We are all one, we are all one". If you are anything like me, I hadn't a clue what that even meant. Honestly, I didn't but then it slowly dawned on me and as I delved deeper, its fundamental truth became evident. As I've mentioned before, energy is everything and everything is energy; so really, the only thing that exists is energy and the intelligence that wields it into whatever it sees fit, just those two things, energy and intelligence, nothing else here, there or anywhere in this beautiful universe of ours, exists.

I think we can all agree that consciousness comes before matter i.e. someone must have a thought about a table before it manifests in front of us. Someone's consciousness thought out every exact detail before one or more people turned the idea of the table into a reality. If we look around us, all we see are things we have built, invented, manifested into existence AND nature. Subsequently, nature must have been brought into our reality by an even greater consciousness than ourselves. The Creator THOUGHT the trees, rivers, mountains, planets and everything else that nature has to offer, into our perceived reality. And we ourselves, along with all the other sentient beings in existence, must have been thought into reality as well. It is our intelligence that allows us to be godlike and manifest our thoughts and ideas into existence. The currency we use to be able to manifest, is the energy that already exists, because, as I've already stated, energy cannot be created or destroyed, it's already HERE, it can only be transferred or transmuted.

This superior intelligence/consciousness that thought us and all the other intelligent life forms into existence, must have also thought energy itself into existence. Though, looking at the state of the world and how we treat each other and the gift that is our planet, it's hugely debatable whether or not we are intelligent.

If the only thing that exists is this superior intelligence i.e. the Creator, then we, along with everything else that is, was or ever will be, stem from said intelligence, created from energy, it itself created.

I have absolutely no idea as to why it created this energy from which we all derive in the first place, I am not smart enough to speculate on that, but I do understand why we are all one. Because only this superior intelligence/ consciousness, the Creator, exists, nothing else and we, along with everything else, are part of it.

Now, if I put my Sherlock Holmes hat on, I could deduce that this superior intelligence thought a finite amount of energy into existence, while placing an infinite number of possibilities on how this energy could be used, hence, energy cannot be created or destroyed only transferred or transmuted and we, with our intelligence, have the capability to tap into this energy and manifest whatever our imagination is capable of thinking up. So basically, we, the world we live in and everything that exists, is inside this energy bubble and we, through the power of our subconscious mind, have the power to tap into this energy and use it for whatever it is we can imagine. Everything already exists as a possibility in this energy bubble. We merely have to reach in and grab it, so to speak.

Becoming Present

Now, how do we access this energy bubble with infinite possibilities and use it to manifest our thoughts?

As I've stated earlier, through the power of our subconscious mind. Our subconscious mind is linked directly to this energy bubble and we, as intelligent beings whose consciousness is divided into two, the conscious mind and the subconscious mind, have the capacity to manifest our dreams and thus become godlike ourselves, by connecting to it through our subconscious mind. To do this, we must be completely in the present moment.

Again, what does it actually mean to be in the present moment? You always hear people going on and on about being present etc, there are whole industries dedicated to this subject matter but what the fuck does it actually mean? Actors are constantly told to just be present, discover the truth, moment to moment and so on.

Being present for me means to be free of thought,

not thinking with your conscious mind, being thought-less i.e. completely in your subconscious!

How do we do that?

There are many ways I'm sure but the one that works for me is through my senses.

Allow me to explain my understanding of it through using an acting example again. All the work an actor does preparing for their role is done using their conscious mind; we learn how to do a particular job, how to handle any number of props, how to speak a certain way, master an accent, ride a horse, move in a precise way and a variety of other things to help us feel as real as possible in our chosen "as if" situation i.e. the scene we are going to be playing in. We have to be very conscious as we program all this information into the computer that is our brain, so that when the actual work begins, we can totally forget about it and be completely in the moment and react through our subconscious mind. Because the part of our consciousness that gets activated between "action and cut", is our subconscious mind. That means, the moment you enter the scene and the director is about to utter the infamous line "action", you are now thought-less and reacting to the stimulus that you are being presented with.

You enter this space by using your senses! What are you seeing? What are you feeling? What are you hearing, smelling etc? You start with your most dominant sense and work your way through them. Through your senses you will become absolutely present and will have switched the position of your conscious mind and your subconscious mind. You will be completely in the latter and now your work will be able to flow and look and feel free and real. By being in your subconscious mind, which we've accessed through our senses, we are now connecting to the energy bubble which holds infinite possibilities and we can reach in and grab our character from within this bubble and manifest it in front of an audience.

Yes, that's right, it already exists as a possibility within the energy bubble.

You can only access this energy bubble and pull down your manifestation if you have left your LEROY and the rest of your conscious mind behind. Allow your senses to put you into your subconscious mind and therefore into complete presence.

Everything that has ever been created through us humans, from architecture to technology to art, already exists as a possibility in this energy bubble, what we have to do is reach in and grab it, that includes all the roles that every actor has ever played or will play in the future.

Originality only exists in the first moment of our witnessing of it, but it's always existed as a possibility within the energy bubble of infinite possibilities.

Originality, like everything else, is an illusion of the ego, Leroy.

We are part of the consciousness that flows through everything, past, present and future. We cannot be separated from it, because nothing but this intelligence exists. We, and everything we create, irrelevant of how minute or large we may perceive it to be, is born out of this intelligence, along with everything we witness that it has created e.g. nature etc.

When we truly realise this, we become totally unfuckable with!

Unfuckable With

A friend of mine first used this phrase and immediately, due to my childish nature, I fell in love with it. Not knowing what it meant straight away, and since it was becoming quite a popular expression over the internet, I felt it behoved me to at least figure out what it means to me, before I started throwing it around.

"Unfuckable with" for me, means to be so at peace with yourself that you become immune to anyone or anything pulling your strings and eliciting a negative emotional response from you. To have reached such a state of Zen that you won't allow anyone to control you by coaxing out a negative response, no matter what was said or done.

It means to be completely free and not hooked to your ego through fear. You're free because nothing can yank your chain and make you go back to feeling those negative emotions that we talked about earlier, ever again.

You have become so PRESENT, that you can stop these emotions from rising and consuming you because you realise in the moment, that we are all one, there is nothing else in existence but this superior intelligence/consciousness that created everything and from which everything stems.

Our life is just a story within a story and sadly not all stories are pleasant ones to be experienced, that is certain. Our job is solely to have the experience and observe and grow without identifying with the experience. The moment we claim ownership of our hardship, successes or anything else for that matter, we have fallen into the trap of the ego and have now distanced ourselves from our true divine nature.

To put it in other terms; there is only the Creator!

Nothing else exists to be unhappy or upset with, other people or things are only providing us with opportunities to grow. We have to detach from the drama our ego feeds off and stay attached to everything that is. All separation is an illusion of the ego which the ego needs to create so that it can stay alive, because the moment you realise your own divinity, your ego ceases to have control over you.

Now, you are truly free from fear and a fearless human is a human who walks side by side with the Creator with love in his heart and cannot be controlled. We are here for the ride, so let's enjoy it while it lasts and stop wasting our time with harbouring negative emotions towards anything or anybody.

The moment we realise who we truly are, we become unfuckable with!

We are all one, we are all connected. Our intelligence allows us to use this energy, which the Creator thought into existence, in any way we choose to see fit. Evil only exists because we allow it into our hearts once we disconnect from our divine nature and connect to our ego, the dark side of the force.

Everywhere you look, whether human, animal, nature or human construct, remember the Creator is looking back at you. Because nothing else exists but this superior intelligence! It is both the light and the dark side of the force and it's your choice who you give your energy to, which determines the experience you will have.

But what tools do we have to stay in a state of Zen, to stay unfuckable with?

Well, by using your superpowers of course. We have many but there are four in my opinion above all else;

Gratitude, forgiveness, love and joy.

Gratitude
Forgiveness   Love
Joy

It is the birth right of every human being to experience joy, in fact we deserve to be in a constant state of joy. Yet life has so many twists and turns that we forget this fact and stay stuck in a loop of suffering until we have convinced ourselves that THIS is what we deserve, it is not! The Creator didn't place us here, so we can stay stuck in a loop of suffering, no, we have done that on our own by following our ego, allowing ourselves to feel separate from the Creator, when we are not. We do this, as I said in a previous chapter, by identifying with our traumas, our hardships, our successes and so on. That is the game our ego plays on us, your Leroy is literally playing you. Whether through the good things or the bad things you perceive to have happened in your life.

So how do we become joyful?

How about we exchange the loop of suffering for another loop?

Before we experience joy, we must first experience love and before we can experience love, we must first experience forgiveness and before that, we must first experience gratitude which then leads us back to joy.

Why not use THIS loop?

These are superpowers after all that are available to every human being on this planet, we all have access to these superpowers and can use them to make our life more joyful.

What's stopping us?

Surely all of us recognise that these are high frequency vibrations that would elevate our consciousness and make us feel capable of achieving tremendous things in the world.

What if there were a trick to using these superpowers? What if it wasn't about projecting them on to other people? What if it all starts with us?

There is a hermetic (secret) law that says,

"As above so below, as within so without".

For our purpose let us focus on "as within so without".

To me, this means that everything I feel on the inside gets projected to the outside and manifests in my perceived outside world. In other words, I must forgive myself for whatever transgressions I think I have committed because the attachment to these transgressions alone already activates my Leroy, as he identifies with it, thinking he is the one who committed the deed, when we now know that only the Creator exists, so in fact it is the Creator, who committed whatever it is we are asking forgiveness for in the first place. All we now have to do, is to feel grateful for having had the experience and embrace it as an opportunity to grow and wholly commit to growing. Allow our hearts to be filled with gratitude for whatever pain we have caused or suffered and use it as a learning experience.

Leroy is pretty clever isn't he? Always finding a way in there to try and keep you stuck in HIS loop.

Once we have forgiven ourselves, we can now forgive other people because we realise who they are in relation to us, there is only the Creator!

When the superpower of forgiveness has been truly activated, love follows as a natural consequence because we realise we are, and always have been, ENOUGH and worthy of love and so as we commit to loving ourselves, love finds us and we perceive the outside world loving us back.

And once the superpower of love fully takes a hold of us, joy is the natural state that follows. How can we not be joyful when all we feel is love for ourselves and having it reciprocated from the outside? Of course, we are now joyful! Well, if you have activated joy and are feeling it inside you and the outside world greets you with joy, then

I would assume there is lots to be grateful for and so the loop begins again and continues on and on.

It all starts and ends with you. You have the power to dictate the experience you're having by choosing, moment to moment through your presence and awareness of us all being one, which side of the force you want to live in.

Connect to your higher self and allow it to guide you, give up your addiction to negativity and loosen Leroy's grip over you.

From here, it's easy to get to "love is the answer no matter what the question". Because deep down you recognise, like the great bard before us;

"All the world's a stage, and all the men and women merely players".

Big Up

Although I write alone, what comes out is in no doubt heavily influenced by the teachers from whom I have been blessed to learn. Long may you continue to allow me to be your student.

To my Kabbalah teacher, mentor and spiritual guide, who coined the phrase "love is the answer no matter what the question" and was gracious enough to allow me to use his beautiful phrase. First, thank you for that and thank you for always holding me to its standard and I apologise for failing you, quite a lot of course, naturally. Though you never judged me or got disheartened with me, instead you remained patient and kept inviting me to join you on the bar you set, waiting for me to get there eventually. Your continued guidance remains a source of strength, thank you.

To my Qi Gong teacher, who introduced me to how energy works and travels in our bodies, fire down water up. Nothing like having a graceful, little lady shouting how weak you are because you can't hold the sleeping tiger position for longer than ten minutes, look it up you'll understand. Thank you for always checking in on my mind too and sharing the tools on how to balance the two sides and get the best out of that beautiful thing we call our brain. You humbled me on so many levels with your grace and patience.

Thank you to my hypnotherapist, for explaining how important those first seven years are in forming our subconscious and the power that our subconscious plays in our everyday lives all the way to the present moment. Thank you, of course, for helping me reconnect again with those long lost.

And a huge thank you to my guruji in India, who guided me through the pandemic, using yoga, breath, mantra, meditation and endlessly shared his wisdom on how to connect to the bigger system. My gratitude towards you is endless.

To anyone who has ever taught me anything, you are all my teachers and unbeknownst to you, have been a huge influence in my life.

Finally, to my family, my wife and kids. The mirror which reflects back to me all that still needs to be ironed out. On a daily basis, your love encourages me and fuels me to be better. I live, I breathe for you.

The Student

Mido Hamada